Book 1:

Single Women & Cars

BY J.J. Jones

&

Book 2:

Single Women & Real Estate

BY J.J. Jones

&

Book 3:

Single Women & Finances

BY J.J. Jones

Book 1:
Single Women & Cars
BY J.J.JONES

Successful Strategies for Searching, Purchasing, and Maintaining Their Car

Finances Box Set #7: Single Women & Cars + Single Women & Real Estate + Single Women & Finances

Copyright 2014 J.J.Jones - All rights reserved.

In no way is it legal to reproduce, duplicate, or transmit any part of this document in either electronic means or in printed format. Recording of this publication is strictly prohibited and any storage of this document is not allowed unless with written permission from the publisher. All rights reserved.

Table Of Contents

Introduction 5

Chapter 1: Single-Women and Their Car Buying Experience 6

Chapter 2: Where to Search for the Right Car 7

Chapter 3: Factors to Consider When Choosing a Car 9

Chapter 4: Car Buying Tips for Single Women 11

Chapter 5: Buying a Brand New Car vs. Used Car 13

Chapter 6: How to Lower the Car's Price 15

Chapter 7: Car Maintenance, Repair, and General Care Tips 17

Conclusion 19

Introduction

I want to thank you and congratulate you for purchasing the book, *"Single Women & Cars: Successful Strategies For Searching, Purchasing, And Maintaining Their Car"*.

This book contains proven steps and strategies on how to search, purchase, and maintain a car if you are a single lady.

It is more challenging for single women to search for a car that suits their needs, go to a car dealership and purchase the car, and maintain the car to keep it in good condition. This is because single women still experience discrimination when it comes to anything that has something to do with cars. It may sound sexist or stereotypical but many car dealer salesmen believe that men are more knowledgeable than women when it comes to cars, the same way that most people think that women are more knowledgeable about makeup and fashion.

If you are a single lady looking to buy a car or who has a car and needs tips and information about repairs and maintenance, you have come to the right place because this book will help you search, purchase, and maintain your car.

Thanks again for purchasing this book, I hope you enjoy it!

Chapter 1: Single-Women and Their Car Buying Experience

Women still experience gender discrimination when it comes to buying cars, which is surprising considering the fact that women buy about 60% of all brand new cars and about 53% of all used cars according to research. This shows that they buy more cars than men, but most car salesmen treat them badly when they go to car dealerships. It's not that they do not assist women buyers or they are rude at them. When women go to a car dealership searching for a new or used car that they want to buy, they are often treated with condescension or patronizing attitude by male salesmen. Many salesmen in car dealerships think that women buying cars are quick and easy transactions that do not require too much effort.

A lot of men think that women do not know much about cars and they often carry this condescending attitude when transacting with women. This results to women thinking and feeling that they don't have a trustworthy salesperson or that they are not being treated fairly. A study also showed that female customers are quoted higher prices than men, because salesmen think that women will easily fall for it because they do not know any better.

Some car dealership companies now promote gender equality by conducting sensitivity trainings. They understand the value of the women's market and that it is business suicide if they provide special treatment to one group of customer and unfair treatment to the other group. However, there are still a lot of car dealers and salesmen who discriminate against women. As a female buyer, you can turn this disadvantage to your advantage by gaining more knowledge and information about cars—what to look for, tips for buying, and maintenance and repair.

These macho salesmen and car dealers automatically think that female buyers like you do not know anything about cars, which will make it easier for you to negotiate because their guard is down. They do not know that you have an idea about pricing, paper work and other important considerations when it comes to buying a car, whether used or brand new. This can also help you avoid scams because you can detect if something is not right based on your acquired knowledge about cars.

By knowing everything there is to know about buying cars, you will be able to shop wisely and get the best deal possible for the kind of car that you need and want.

The next few chapters will provide you with some practical tips and information about finding the right car, buying and negotiating with the dealer, and repair and maintenance.

Chapter 2: Where to Search for the Right Car

You need to know where you can find cars for sale if you are planning to buy one. By knowing the best places to find cars for sale, you will have more options in terms of the type, quality, and price of cars. There are a number of great places where you can find cars for sale. You can check out the list below.

Car dealerships

This is the best source of brand new and used cars. These are local car distributors that have a dealership contract with a car company, especially if they are selling brand new cars. Car dealerships have salespeople working for them and they are the ones who assist you when you make a visit and want to look at their available cars for sale. Most car dealerships also provide maintenance and repair services for brand new cars. They have their own team of automotive technicians and mechanics who repair damages that are covered by the warranty and who sell replacement parts. Car dealerships need to follow rules such as selling their cars at reasonable prices and disclosing details about the car that the buyer needs to know, which makes it safer for buyers like you.

Online car websites

There are also a lot of websites that sell both brand new and used cars. These are simply like online car dealerships. They have a list of all the cars they have available for sale and important information and details about the car such as make and model, mileage, and price. They also provide a picture that the buyer can view. It is important that all the basic details of the car are available in the website so that you will have an idea if they have what you are looking for before you try to contact them. One advantage of browsing for available cars for sale online is the convenience. You can browse through different car websites in one sitting and only visit those that have the kind of car that you are searching for. the drawback is that there is no immediate response to your answer unless you call them or you visit their showroom personally.

Online supermarkets

You can also buy cars, especially used cars, from online supermarkets like eBay and Craigslist. Here, you can find individual sellers who are selling their own cars for a variety of reasons. Some are selling their old cars because they are planning to buy a new one while others just need to dispose of their car for the money. When buying from individual sellers online, you have to be careful because some of these are scammers who prey on people who are not knowledgeable enough about cars and online buying. It is important not to make any payments until you meet up with the seller. For local listings, Craigslist is the best option. But if you are looking for rare vintage cars, eBay is the best place to go.

From people you know

You can also buy a car from someone you know, like a friend or coworker. This is not only convenient but also very safe because you are dealing with someone you know and trust. You can even haggle for a lower price if you are buying the car from a close friend or a relative. If you do not yet have money to pay for the car in full, you can ask your friend if you can make your payment in installment. The only downside is that you have limited choices because you are only dealing with people around you.

Chapter 3: Factors to Consider When Choosing a Car

After knowing where you can search for available cars for sale, you should now learn how to choose the right car for a single lady like you. You need to understand that different individuals and car buyers have different needs when it comes to cars. A family with children needs a bigger car for all those family picnics and trips while a single man or woman needs a smaller car because they do not have any children to drive around. To learn more tips about this, you can check out the following paragraphs.

Size

As what has been mentioned earlier, a single woman like you only requires a small car because you do not need to ferry around kids or your whole family. You will most likely use the car to go to work and run some personal errands. It is not practical to buy an SUV or a pickup which is too big for your needs. It is not only more expensive, but it is also more difficult to park, especially if you live in a large city like New York where owning a car, especially a big car, is more trouble than it's worth. Moreover, driving a large vehicle makes it more difficult for you to weave in and out of traffic. So unless you need to carry a large group of passengers or some bulky equipment on a regular basis, you can choose a small two-seater sports car or a hatchback with a small compartment.

Budget

You also need to consider your budget when buying a car. Single women may have fewer responsibilities than married women but this does not mean that they can splurge all they want. You still need to be practical when buying a car in terms of the price. You do not want to spend all your savings on buying a car which you will replace after a few years. Single women and men alike also need to save money in case they want to have a family of their own in the future. You need to save up enough money for the car that you are planning to buy. When you visit a dealership, you should remember the amount that you have set and stick to it no matter what. You should look for cars that are within your budget so that you do not have to loan money or apply for financing when buying a car.

Reliability

You need to choose a car that is reliable. This means that the car should be in good condition and will not break down on you all the time. It is troublesome and expensive to buy a car that is always in need of repair. You also do not want your car to break down while you are driving it to work or while you are in the middle of doing something important. Like buying a pair of shoes or a bag, choose a car that will last a long time and will give you your money's worth.

Safety

Single women should also look for safety features when it comes to buying a car. The car should have automatic locks that will protect you while you are inside. It should also have an airbag that will protect you in the event of a car crash and you are driving alone and no one is there to help you immediately. You can also choose a car with sensors and cameras that will make driving in a highway, parking, and backing out so much easier and safer.

Chapter 4: Car Buying Tips for Single Women

You need to understand that what single women need to know when buying a car is just the same as what single men or even married individuals need to know. You need to know the same information about the car and you need to look out for the same things. The only difference is the way women are treated in car dealerships when buying a car. This is why it is essential that you go to the car dealership well-prepared so that these sexist salesmen will not have a chance to treat you unfairly. Below is a list of car buying tips that every single woman should know.

Know what you want before going to the dealership

You should already have an idea about the kind of car you want to buy based on your needs and preferences. You need to have a number of makes and models in mind that suit your budget. This way, the salesman will know that you already know what you want and will not show you other vehicles that do not really suit your needs but will give them a huge bonus.

You need to do some research about the car that you want such as the features and other details of the car. This way, you will know if they are telling you everything you need to know or if they are withholding something. The price is also an important detail that you need to know. Researching about the car's price will also give you an idea how much you should be paying for a specific make and model. You can then decide to transact with the car dealership that lays out all the details and information about the car and gives you a reasonable price for it.

This way, you will know if they are telling you everything you need to know or if they are withholding something.

Decide on a budget and stick to it

Some car dealers think that women buyers tend to overspend. This is because society depicts some women as shopaholics who do not have control over their spending habits. They also think that women are attracted to anything that looks shiny, smooth, and sleek. They will try to give you something that looks really great but is well beyond your budget. When you first visit the car dealer, you need to state your budget right away and tell the salesman that you are only looking for cars that are within your budget and that he should not waste his time showing you other more expensive cars.

Let the car dealer know that you mean business

The salesperson or car dealer will not take you seriously if you giggle and gush whenever you are shown a car that looks cute. It is difficult to take a female buyer seriously if she is acting like a schoolgirl. And instead of playing dumb to get what you want, like what some women do, you need to make sure that the car dealer or salesman knows that you did your homework and you are informed. This way, the salesman will go straight to the point and will give you the important details and features of the car without wasting your time on insignificant features like the color of the seat fabric or how the sleek design fits you perfectly. You should ask intelligent questions like horsepower, gas efficiency, warranty, and past damages for used cars that will let the salesperson know that you know your stuff and that you are not someone to mess with.

Bring a mechanic with you

Men also bring a mechanic with them if they are not confident about their knowledge about cars. You can bring a trusted mechanic who can take a look at the car and give you important details that you need to know. Bringing a mechanic with you will also make the salesman treat you like a male customer when doing transactions. It may seem contradictory to hire a man when you are proving that women can do it, but you sometimes need to take certain actions to prove a point. Let the mechanic give you the information about the car's engine and other important details but show them that the final decision is still up to you.

Chapter 5: Buying a Brand New Car vs. Used Car

This is the question that many car buyers are asking. They want to know the pros and cons of buying a brand new car versus buying a used car. You will learn about the details in this chapter to help you decide whether to buy a used or a brand new car.

Pros of buying a brand new car

- *It's not used.* If you buy a brand new car, you will be the first owner. It does not have damage or accident history from the past, it does not have a funny smell, and it is clean and in excellent brand new condition.
- *Customizable.* You can also customize the car's features according to your needs and preferences. A lot of car companies allow their buyers to customize the car that they are planning to buy in terms of color and other features.
- *Warranty.* A brand new car's warranty is untouched and there is no need to pay extra because it is included in the package when you paid for the car.
- *Latest technology.* Your brand new car will also have the modern technology features that will make driving it more fun and exciting. If you are a techie or a geek, you will surely enjoy driving a car that has all the latest gizmos.
- *Safety.* Safety standards imposed by different organizations for car manufacturers change all the time. If you buy a brand new car, you can be sure that it follows all the required safety procedures and standards. Otherwise, their cars will be pulled out which means profit losses for them.

Cons of buying a brand new car

- *Expensive.* A brand new car is a lot more expensive than a used car. This is the main reason many people choose to buy second hand cars.
- *Depreciation.* A brand new car loses its value right after being driving out from the dealer's lot. Imagine the depreciation after a few years and the first owner is the one who has to shoulder the depreciation.

Pros of buying a used car

- *Cheap.* Used cars are by far cheaper than brand new cars. This allows you to find a nicer model that suits your budget.
- *Low insurance.* Insurance rates are lower for used cars than brand new cars. This is because if a used car gets damaged, it is cheaper to have it repaired than if a brand new car is damaged.
- *More choices.* If you are the type of person who prefers old model cars and vintage cars, you should definitely buy second hand because brand new cars only have the latest models. Some people prefer old cars than the

sleek and futuristic looking new models that car manufacturers make these days.

Cons of buying a used car

- **Used.** You will not be the first owner if you buy a used car. The car may have been in an accident or may have undergone major repairs and fixed. You should manage your expectations when buying a used car because there will surely be a flaw no matter how small.
- **Mileage.** This is the number of miles that the car has run during its lifetime. The larger the mileage, the more used the car is.

Basically, it is still up to you whether you should buy a brand new car or a used car. If money is not an issue, then you should go for a brand new car. But if you have a limited budget or you simply do not want to spend a lot of money on buying a car, then you should go for a used car that is still in good condition.

Chapter 6: How to Lower the Car's Price

With everything you have learned about how car dealers and salesmen give female buyers a higher quote than male buyers, you need to learn some tactics that will help you lower the car's price. Here are some tactics for getting the best deal.

Don't negotiate

If you have found what you are looking for but the price is a little over your budget, do not negotiate with the car dealer. Tell them that you will sign the documents and make the purchase once they hit your target price amount or once they have something available that is within your budget. Decline any offers that they will give you. Just leave them your phone number and leave. They are bound to call you, especially if the car has been sitting there for a long time.

Find the right timing

There are certain times of the month or year when car dealers lower their price. For example, the last day of the month puts a lot of pressure on salespeople and managers because they have to meet their quota. They are more willing to lower their price if it means one more sale for them before the end of the month. They are in a hurry to meet their quota. And for them, it is better to hit their monthly quota and avoid a lecture from the big boss than to get a huge commission. They can get a commission some other time but they might not be able to find another well-paying job.

They are also more willing to lower their price after a terrible weather when sales are low and there are very few potential buyers. After all, no want is probably thinking about buying a car when they need to clean up their house or yard after a storm or blizzard.

Always be polite

Do not threaten the car dealer by telling them that you will do business somewhere else because they will only react in a negative way which will make it more difficult for you to haggle. Instead, turn on the charm and be polite so that the car dealer or salesperson will find it difficult to say no.

Know how much the car is worth

It is easier to lower the price if you know how low you can go to buy the car. For brand new cars, you can visit TrueCar.com or Edmunds.com for an estimate on the car's worth. You can also use Kelley's Blue Book for the value of both new and used cars.

Be prepared to walk away

Do not buy a car on impulse or just because you feel sorry for the sales rep who still has to meet his quota. Do not also agree to any price that you are not comfortable with just because you think you are losing a deal. If the deal is not going your way and it is not something that you like, you should be ready to walk away. Remind yourself that there are so many other cars and dealers out there and you can try to find your luck somewhere else.

Chapter 7: Car Maintenance, Repair, and General Care Tips

Men may be more interested in tinkering with car engines but women can also do the same thing if they put their mind to it. Some women are simply not interested in cars and this is the main reason why they lack the knowledge and skills for maintaining and repairing a car. It does not mean that they are less intelligent. They are just not interested, the same way that most men are not interested about fashion and therefore do not know a lot of thing about fashion.

To give you some tips for car maintenance, repair, and general care, you can check out the short list below.

General care tips

- *Wash your car regularly.* If you use your car every day, you should also wash it regularly to remove dirt, grime, acid rain, smoke, dead bugs, bird poop, dust, and other dirt debris that can eat away your car's paint. You need to wash your car two or three times a month especially if you live in a polluted area or near the sea.
- *Don't throw trash inside your car.* Many people turn their car into a moving garbage bin. Clean the inside of your car by removing crumpled papers and empty bottles. You should also vacuum the flooring and seat regularly.
- *Clean the windshield.* Cleaning the windshield does not only make your car look nice. It also prevents accidents because your view of the road is not obscured by dead bugs or bird poop. You should also clean your headlights using a soft sponge or a squeegee.
- *Clean your engine.* Your engine also acquires dirt and grime and it is important to give your car an engine wash at least once a year. You can bring your car to a car wash shop or you can do it yourself. Just make sure that you know which engine parts should be protected from water.

Maintenance tips

- *Change your engine oil and filter regularly.* A used car requires more frequent oil change than a brand new car. Changing your car's engine oil flushes out dirt and particles out of the engine. This clears the exhaust that comes out of the tailpipe and makes the car run smoothly. You should also replace your old filter when you change your engine oil because you do not want the clean oil to mix with the dirt coming from the old filter.
- *Check your tire pressure.* Always keep your tires inflated at the recommended pressure. You can find this in your car's manual or near the

driver's seat. You should also check for wheel realignment to prevent uneven tire wear. Other causes of uneven tire wear are worn out shock absorbers or brakes, or damage in the internal tire or a bent wheel.
- *Change sparkplugs.* To ensure fuel efficiency and better engine performance, you need to change your spark plugs every 50,000 km.
- *Take care of your car battery.* To extend the life of your car battery, you should always keep the terminal clean by wiping it with a dam rag. You should also look out for cracks and bulges that will tell you if you need to replace your battery.
- *Have the brakes inspected.* Just like the soles of your shoes, brake shoes also become worn out when used on a regular basis. When damaged, this can lead to damage to the brake rotor which is more expensive to repair.
- *Learn how to check vital fluids.* There are five fluids that you need to check to ensure safety while driving—oil, coolant or anti-freeze, brake fluid, transmission fluid, and windshield wiper fluid.

Repair tips

- *Repair minor damages right away.* If you can hear a weird sound while driving or if you find something amiss when you open the hood to check the engine, you should have it checked right away to prevent it from getting worse. If there is a minor damage, it is best to fix it immediately to prevent unnecessary extra costs.
- *Learn to change a flat tire.* This is one of the most basic repair processes that you need to know. Learn how to use the lug wrench and jack so that when you get stranded in the middle of nowhere because of a flat tire, you can simply change the tire yourself.
- *Keep a toolbox or bag in your car.* You need to bring tools that will help you fix damages while on the road like screwdrivers, cutting pliers, jack, lug wrench, torque wrench, ratchet driver, channel locks, work light, and so on.
- *Be comfortable under the hood.* Some women do not like the idea of going under the hood to check or repair the car. This is why they just decide to simply bring the car to a nearby mechanic who can fix it for them, but will cost them hundreds of dollars. This is why you need to be comfortable under the hood to be able to do even the major fixes yourself. You can ask someone to teach you about car maintenance and repair or you can watch videos or read articles online.
- *Go to a professional mechanic.* If the damage is beyond your knowledge and skills, you have no other choice but to go to a mechanic. A professional mechanic can help you with just about any car trouble but be prepared to pay more than if you do it yourself.

Conclusion

Thank you again for purchasing this book!

I hope this book was able to help you to learn some useful tips and information about searching, buying, and maintaining a car for single women like you.

The next step is to apply what you have learned from this book if you are planning to buy your own car.

Finally, if you enjoyed this book, please take the time to share your thoughts and post a review on Amazon. We do our best to reach out to readers and provide the best value we can. Your positive review will help us achieve that. It'd be greatly appreciated!

Thank you and good luck!

Book 2:
Single Women & Real Estate:
BY J.J.JONES

Successful Tips A Woman Needs To Search, Negotiate, and Purchase Their Own Home

Finances Box Set #7: Single Women & Cars + Single Women & Real Estate + Single Women & Finances

Copyright 2014 J.J.Jones - All rights reserved.

In no way is it legal to reproduce, duplicate, or transmit any part of this document in either electronic means or in printed format. Recording of this publication is strictly prohibited and any storage of this document is not allowed unless with written permission from the publisher. All rights reserved.

Finances Box Set #7: Single Women & Cars + Single Women & Real Estate + Single Women & Finances

Table Of Contents

Introduction 23

Chapter 1 The Trend In Real Estate Today.. 24

Chapter 2 Location, Location, Location.. 26

Chapter 3 A Single Woman's Dream House.......................................27

Chapter 4 Home Buying Guide For Single Women........................... 29

Chapter 5 The Importance of Hiring A Real Estate Agent 31

Chapter 6 What To Do After Buying A Home.................................... 33

Conclusion 34

Introduction

I want to thank you and congratulate you for purchasing the book, *"Single Women & Real Estate: Successful Tips A Woman Needs To Search, Negotiate, and Purchase Their Own Home"*.

This book contains proven steps and strategies on how single women can purchase their dream homes without too much effort and mistakes.

According to the latest surveys, an estimated 21% of homebuyers are single women. With this trend, the homebuilders are designing homes that would appeal to the lady buyers. To find the right home specifically addressing the needs of the single ladies, here are some successful tips as guide. However, this book contains more than that. It would also assist single women on topics such as why women buy homes, assessing financial status, the importance of hiring a real estate agent, and so much more!

Thanks again for purchasing this book, I hope you enjoy it!

Chapter 1 The Trend In Real Estate Today

Single women are dominating the real estate industry by being the leaders of homebuyers today. To be precise, these ladies are causing the growth of real estate business by making up almost 1/3 of sales since 1944. Next to them are married couples. Compared to single men, single women are twice more likely to buy a home. With this trend, homebuilders are designing the houses suitable to meet the single women's needs. The forecast of real estate analysts is that this trend will continue in the coming years.

Reasons why single women are buying homes

Included among single women are the divorced, widows, and the unmarried. One might wonder why these women are spending so much of their money and savings to secure a house. Well, here are some of the reasons why:

- ➢ Rent is more expensive. In reality, renting is less stressful for a single woman. She does not have to worry about repairs, upkeeps, property taxes and monthly mortgages when she is just renting a place. Those are the responsibilities of the landlord. However, in the long run, renting would be more expensive than buying and maintaining a house. If for instance her rent is between $1000 to $1500 per month, she would be able to find a monthly mortgage close enough to this amount. By paying a down-payment that is a little higher than the usual, her mortgage would even be sometimes lower than the rent. Plus, she owns the property, unlike if she is just a renter.
- ➢ Women are high earners now. Unlike in ancient times when women were not educated and were not allowed to work as CEO's or in higher positions, the women workers today enjoy the same privileges as the male workers. Additionally, they are also given credits and loans now. Are you aware that it was only in the mid 1900's that the women were allowed to loan without a male guarantor? Even if she had a good career and savings, she would not be given a loan without a male guaranteeing her loan. Credit cards were difficult to be approved too, if you were a female, back then. Today, that has changed. Studies even reveal that women are better in managing their finances than men. They are also more committed in paying their loans than the males.
- ➢ They prefer to relocate somewhere nearer to their work or school. It could be because of practicality or tendency to physically tire out easily compared to men, but one of the factors why single women's buy homes is to be near their office or school. Location of the property is therefore, a primary concern.
- ➢ Women want to invest.It is like hitting two birds with one stone. Women need to have their own place plus they are aware that real estate is a good investment. Put that together and you would understand why many single women are buying homes. Single women need the financial security that owning a home brings. Even if there is an economic crisis, a single woman who has a home would be less anxious knowing that she would not be

thrown out of her own house or she could sell the house if she needs to. There is even an opportunity to earn when one has a home. The single woman could rent to others the extra rooms in the house.

- It is her tendency to nest. Women are known as the homemakers. They just love to decorate the rooms of the house and do improvements as much as they can. They could get attached to a home more easily than the other gender. This is why they buy their own instead of just rent. They want to give the house their own personal touches, which is possible if they own the place themselves. Otherwise, there could be additional charges or issues with the landlords if they are just renters.
- Women want to be independent. Women have truly evolved. From being the clingy, dependent creatures they were portrayed to be centuries ago, they have now become independent and self-reliant. They have also pursued education and have focused on their careers. More and more women are delaying marriage or totally forgo it. Gone are the days where the lady waits for her prince charming and expects him to provide her a house. Nowadays, ladies buy their own houses and sometimes, live on their own for the rest of their lives...and they still live happily ever after.

In the following chapters, finding the perfect house for a single lady would be done easily with these proven steps. The first priority is finding the perfect location before the perfect house. Discover the best place to purchase a house for a single woman.

Chapter 2 Location, Location, Location

You have probably heard the number one tip in buying a house or any property for that matter – the first is location, the 2nd and 3rd tip is still location. This is to emphasize how important location is. You may have the perfect house, but if the premises are surrounded by hazardous elements such as factories emitting toxic gases, then that is a no-no. Or maybe, the place is near the airport and every day, you would encounter the loud engines of airplanes taking off, again that would not be the ideal place to experience serenity and peace. If you find the perfect location but the house is not the one you like, it is the better option. You could always renovate the house. On the other hand, it would be hard or even impossible to do anything about the surroundings. The bottom line – if you have to choose, choose the one with the better location.

What do women need?

Single women have special needs when it comes to buying homes. However, the two most important things to consider are the following:

1. Proximity to loved ones, work or school and other important establishments. Although they live alone and they want to be independent, single women still prefer to be in close contacts with friends and families. They would choose a house not too far away from where they loved ones live. Unless, the distance of the new home would take them away from their work or job, that is. Then they would choose the one nearer their work area. Usually, they would just visit the family on weekends. They have to report at work more often than visit the family, hence the choice. Also, single women are concerned whether there are hospitals, grocery stores, transportation systems, police stations, other important establishments nearby. Living solo, they want to have easy access to essential authorities, any time of the day.
2. Safety and Security. As they are living on their own, a very important feature of the location is its safety. A good tip to do is to check the crime rate of the city. To be more specific, you could also visit the nearest police station and check the incidences of crime in that particular community that you are interested in. It is also advisable that you bring a camera and take photos of the surrounding buildings or communities on your way to the new place. That way, you could check in details the important factors that would contribute to the total safety of the place. Check if it is a gated community. For single women, this feature is a big point as it can guarantee lesser occurrences of robbery and break in. Pay attention, too for the presence of good lighting system in the community. A well-lighted place is less prone for crime and other violence.

When these two basic requirements are met, other minor details are acceptable even if their preferences are not totally met. When the issue of the location is dealt with, the next thing to consider is the feature of the house itself. Find out what single women really like when it comes to their homes.

Chapter 3 A Single Woman's Dream House

The needs of single women are unique when it comes to houses. Not to stereotype women, but it has been noted that they tend to change their minds over every little thing, every now and then. However, when it comes to the features of the house, they seem to stick to certain attributes. They have specific details of what makes a dream house. What are these?

1. Again, safety, and security. It is not enough that the neighborhood (or even the city itself) is very safe. The dream house must be safe and secure, too. How?
    a. An attached gate is preferable. The one with an electronic garage door opener is the most ideal. Why? Many reports show that attacks against women happen while they are parking their cars or opening their front doors. To prevent this from happening, this safety feature of a garage is highly recommendable. The woman would not need to go out of her car to get inside the house. Plus, once the garage door is secured, she could open the door without fear of anyone behind her.
    b. Another is the installation of the security system of the house itself. The latest home security system would include not only monitoring and immediate reporting of burglary, but also medical alert monitoring. Usually, there is a connected device on the security system that the woman can use to ask for help in the event of a medical emergency. There are also features such as fire and smoke alert, temperature and flood monitoring, and sometimes even carbon monoxide monitoring.
    c. Doors and windows. There are two ways where most of the robbers enter the house – through the doors and windows. That is why, for single women, assessment of the quality of doors and windows comes as a priority. The doors should not be jammed. They should be heavy built. They should be the type that would not open by just kicking it forcefully. The knobs should not have any sign of damage, as well. As for the windows, it should also be very sturdy. If it is glass, it should be the double-glass windowpanes. The lock should be away from the glass part too so that even if the robber would break the glass, he would not be able to reach for the lock. Screens could serve as protection, too and not just to prevent insects from coming in.
    d. Location of the master bedroom. Most prefer the master bedroom to be in the ground floor (if it is two story or three) for the following reasons: First, they would be able to hear any sound coming from the door or windows in the first floor. Unlike if they are staying upstairs, the chance of hearing any noise is lessened due to the distance. Second, in case of emergency like fire or earthquake, they

would be able to get out of the house more easily. Third, as they grow older, it would be more difficult to climb the stairs.
   e. Fenced backyard. As an added security feature, there is lesser likelihood of robbers climbing a fence just to break in. Therefore, if there is a gated fence or backyard, this is also a big consideration for buying the house. Usually, these single women also procure pets, like dogs, not only as companions but also as added safety measures. According to surveys, those homeowners with dogs experience lesser incidents of break-ins than those without.
2. Cleaning-friendly features. Single women are indeed busy people. They work and keep houses simultaneously. Some even continue their post grad education at the same time. This is why they look for houses that are low maintenance or better yet, no maintenance at all. The floors should be very easy to clean. There should be no elaborate cleaning styles needed. Houses with built in vacuums are getting popular. Tucked away in a small cabinet, the woman has easy access to the vacuum cleaner when needed. Usually, it is located where it can reach all parts of the house, making cleaning easier to accomplish. Some prefer the laundry area to be upstairs, far away from the prying eyes of visitors.
3. Provision for a family later on, in case they marry or have kids. The house should be convertible to a family house in the event that they do decide to get married and have a family of their own. It must have extra spaces for additional rooms or renovations. Women tend to plan ahead compared to men. Although they buy houses ahead of time, they make sure that it would also accommodate "future tenants" when the time comes.
4. Possibility of an income. Single women are typically cautious. They like to be ready for anything. In the event that they lose their jobs or there is an economic crisis, they would like the house to be income generating, too. Usually, they look for a property where there is a separate room that other people could rent. It serves a double purpose, too. Not only do they earn from it, but it also provides company for them, making them feel more secure and safer.

These features make up the dream house of the single ladies. They may see the dream house on their first trip but they would not buy it that time. However, they would surely go back to it after scouting several houses. Maybe, this is how they come to have the "Red Shoe" phenomenon. In this situation, while shopping for a pair of red shoe, when they see the perfect pair, they would leave it and look around other shops. Finally, after several hours, they would return to the perfect pair and buy it.

Now that they have found the right location and the ideal house, it is time to negotiate. Learn some tips on how to go about in negotiating and finally, buying the house.

Chapter 4 Home Buying Guide For Single Women

A home is a major purchase. It warrants enough time of study and research before plunging in. Here are some helpful tips to guide the single women when purchasing a home:

1. Assess one's financial status. Buying a home is not like buying a pair of shoes. One cannot just return it when she realizes she does not like it or does not have enough money to pay for it. Unless one has the money to buy the abode in cash, she would expect to go through a lot of paperwork to secure a loan and she would have to talk to many people. It is an investment of her time and money. The best thing one could do is to sit down with a bank personnel or a real estate broker to determine how much she can afford. Determine also how much one can borrow through the help of a mortgage broker. This is the person who could help the solo buyer maximize her borrowing powers. The single homebuyer should plan the details of her down-payment, monthly mortgages, and other expenses associated with acquiring a house like different taxes, moving expenses, and repairs or renovations. One very good tip to bear in mind is that one should not go beyond what is comfortable in a monthly repayment. Unless there is financial evidence that she can really afford to buy a house, then she should not do so. Otherwise, it would be better for her to remain with her family or rent while she saves some more money.
2. Talk to family and friends about the plan. There is nothing wrong with asking and learning from family and friends on how to purchase a house. Unlike married women who have their partners to consult with about the purchase, single ladies have nobody to share this "challenge" with. Arrange a time of dialogue especially to those who have made home purchases, too. They would be able to share their experiences and give the single homebuyers insight on how to go about the purchase. Ask around and get some recommendations on things like real estate brokers, good neighborhoods, loans, and others.
3. Find and hire a professional real estate broker. Single woman homebuyer should find a real estate agent who is female, single and successful, just like she is. There is a more detailed discussion about real estate broker in the next chapter.
4. Choose the location. Write down the list of the features of the community that one wish to settle down in. Make a checklist to see if the community has what you are looking for. Plus, check the proximity of the house from the office, school, family, and other important establishments such as police station, grocery stores, hospitals, to name just a few.
5. Write down the features of the house that you want. Again, you can make a checklist of what you want. How many rooms and bathrooms do you prefer? Should there be a backyard? How secured is the house?

6. Start the search. Looking online is a great way to help speed up finding that dream house. Checking the local newspapers is also good. You could also register with real estate agents to help you with your search. Do not be frustrated when you do not initially find the house of your dreams. This could take a while. After all, this could be the biggest financial outlay that you would make, so take your time. Do not rush it. When you find something that you like, ask for a schedule of viewing.
7. Make an offer. The seller is used to having buyers asking for discounts and other freebies. Inform the seller how much you can afford. If the seller is willing, he or she would give in to your offer. However, if not, the two of you would try to come to an agreement where both parties are satisfied. A special tip is to never go beyond what you can conveniently pay every month. Sometimes, one can be tempted to go beyond the original computation of the budget. In the end, this would put such a burden on the buyer. Take heed, therefore.
8. Get pre-approved for a mortgage. One of the most important things in buying a house is finding the right loan and lender. Search which lender is best for one's needs. Check the financial report before you submit it to the mortgage broker. Most of the time, the loan is approved due to the previous financial history report. A pre-approved mortgage is important. Usually, the seller favors the buyer with a pre-approved mortgage. When you and the seller have reached an agreement, the paperwork would start. The buyer can ask the solicitor to start working on the contract.
9. Surveying the value of the property. At this point, the lender should arrange for a surveyor. The solo buyer should also arrange for her own surveyor to see other problems. However, she could save money when she asks the same surveyor to do the lender and survey together. Read and study the results of the survey. If she does not find anything wrong with it, then she could go ahead and close the deal. Otherwise, she has to inform the seller as soon as possible of her decision to withdraw from the transaction to avoid incurring penalties.
10. Closing of the sale. There would be a signing of the contract and paying of the down-payment, as per agreement. The date would also be set on which the buyer could transfer in her new home.
11. Renovations, repairs before moving in. She should finalize everything about the security system and renovations needed before she books a moving van. She should also start packing her things and move on the scheduled date.
12. Insure the new property. This is to safeguard the house and its contents in the events of fires, robbery or other disasters.

That's it! The single woman can now enjoy her dream house. Buying a home is not easy but if these steps were followed, then that single lady would come out satisfied with her purchase.

Chapter 5 The Importance of Hiring A Real Estate Agent

One of the most common advices that single, female homebuyers would hear is that they need to hire a professional real estate agent. Why? Here are 10 reasons to ponder:

1. Real estate agents do 80% of the job. If you want a "painless" real estate transaction, then hire a professional real estate agent. They could assist you from day one of the transaction until the very last day. You would also save time, effort and money when you avail of their services. As a working single lady, this is indeed an advantage as you are very busy both with work and personal life. Instead of running around and looking at all the offers, the agent could cut the trips to only those which she thinks would appeal to you.
2. They have the education and experience. These people know the ins and outs of real estate. If this is your first time to buy, you could get lost with the jargons and paper works to be done. They, in turn, know everything there is to know in buying your house and having the best deal. They are also trained on the legal matters of house buying.
3. They can protect you. They are like buffers who would take the initial lashing so that you would be protected from unpleasant experiences. They could show you the positive and negative sides of the property. They could protect you from false information regarding properties.
4. They know the data on market conditions. Real estate agents know how much is the average per square foot, or the average sale prices in a particular neighborhood or ratios of listed and sold houses. These bits of info can help you determine if the community is a good one to invest your money in or not.
5. They can recommend other professionals you may need. These agents can hand you a list of whom to contact when you need a specific professional to do something regarding your buying a home. Examples are the mortgage broker, movers, carpenters, plumbers, and legal officers. They are usually aware of who are the efficient and trustworthy people to recommend to others.
6. They know the neighborhood well. They can tell you who bought which house and who lives next door. They can also tell you how safe or not the community is. They know which person to contact to give you information on these things. Contrary to what is known about agents, they are not just after the commissions. The reason for this is because they would only survive in this industry if they have a good record among clients. Word by mouth referral is still the way to survive for these agents. That is why they give their best to all the clients.

7. They can answer your questions. Single homebuyers are most often bombarded with questions that only the real estate agent can answer, especially those regarding legal issues.
8. They can handle the paperwork. This is actually the hard, and sometimes expensive, part. There are many forms to fill, contracts to read and sign, and documents to submit. Your agent can help you with these. You cannot afford to miss or overlook one. It can be costly in the end. Your agent would double-check all the documents to ensure that you are protected from any legal liability.
9. Concerns even after the sale. Real estate agents do not disappear once the deal is closed. You can still depend on them to assist you even after the sale is done. There may be instances of confusion such as tax transfer, document stamps or property tax assessment. You can call your agent and they would be ready to clarify the confusion easily.
10. For future transactions. Real estate agents know that your paths would meet again, either through a new sale or your referral. This is usually why they build close relationships with clients. In the end, they would become not only as your agents but as your friends as well.

Hiring a professional real estate agent is one good decision. It would lead you to having a pleasant real estate transaction.

Chapter 6 What To Do After Buying A Home

Finally, all paper works are done with. You have the keys to your new abode. What to do after the deal is closed? Here are reminders on what to do before you move in to your dream house:

1. As security is very important to single ladies, change all the locks and keys. If there is a security system, change the password.
2. Pest-proof your new place by calling and having over the exterminator. Secure your new home from pests before you move in. That way, you would not be there when the harsh chemicals are sprayed all over the place. Plus, these pests are more difficult to control when all your things are already there.
3. Take a day or two to clean the house thoroughly before you start living there. An empty house is easier to clean, actually. You could also hire a cleaning service if you are pressed for time.
4. Pack and label your things. Protect the fragile items by packing them in padded boxes. This way, you would easily locate the items that you need. Aside from these, pack a small bag with all the toiletries and change of clothing for a day or two. Also secure your important documents. Bring them in your car when you transfer or else they might get lost in the process of transferring. Make a list of your things. This will save you time in the future. As soon as all the boxes are transferred, check your list and see if everything is in there.
5. You do not have to unpack all at once. You could do it by sections or by rooms. Usually, the master bedroom or more specifically, the bed is the first one to be arranged. One important thing to do, however, is to hang your curtains as soon as you arrive so that when nighttime comes, you would have the privacy that you need. If you plan to have Venetian blinds, you should have them installed prior to moving in.
6. You could also start meeting the neighbors. Try to befriend them or just introduce yourself.
7. Relax and have fun. You have erased one item from your bucket list. Revel in this reality. Pat yourself in the back. Smile and take a break from all your work. After all, you deserve it!

Congratulations on your purchase! Enjoy your dream house today!

Conclusion

Thank you again for purchasing this book!

I hope this book was able to help you find that dream house and purchase it.

The next step is to decorate that house to your heart's desire and enjoy living in it, that is, until your next new purchase.

Finally, if you enjoyed this book, please take the time to share your thoughts and post a review on Amazon. We do our best to reach out to readers and provide the best value we can. Your positive review will help us achieve that. It'd be greatly appreciated!

Thank you and good luck!

Book 3:
Single Women & Finances
BY J.J.JONES

A Woman's Secret Diary To Saving, Budgeting, and Retirement

Finances Box Set #7: Single Women & Cars + Single Women & Real Estate + Single Women & Finances

Copyright 2014 by J.J. Jones - All rights reserved.

In no way is it legal to reproduce, duplicate, or transmit any part of this document in either electronic means or in printed format. Recording of this publication is strictly prohibited and any storage of this document is not allowed unless with written permission from the publisher. All rights reserved.

Table of Contents

Introduction 38

Chapter 1: Advantages and Disadvantages of Being a Single Woman.. 39

Chapter 2: Saving Tips for a Single Woman........................ 41

Chapter 3: Budget Tips for the Single Woman................... 43

Chapter 4: Retirement Tips for the Single Woman 45

Chapter 5: Excellent Finance Tips for Women 48

Conclusion 50

Check Out My Other Books 51

Introduction

I want to thank you and congratulate you for purchasing the book, "Single Women & Finances: A Woman's Secret Diary To Saving, Budgeting, and Retirement"

This book contains proven steps and strategies on how to be financially secure in the future.

Because more and more women are opting to become single and enjoy their independence, this book empowers them to take better control of their finances so that they enjoy their lives even when they retire. It takes single women to a journey of saving, budgeting, and retirement planning. This book shares some great and practical tips so that single women enjoy their lives without draining their purses and bank accounts.

Thanks again for purchasing this book, I hope you enjoy it!

Chapter 1: Advantages and Disadvantages of Being a Single Woman

For the 21st Century, being single can equate to happiness and satisfaction. Currently, a lot of women opt to stay single. Marriage is no longer considered a necessity. The woman of today isn't afraid of not having a husband. Today, she can even have a home and a child without a man in her life. Although cultures differ, more and more women have embraced a solitary life.

A single woman is more physically fit because she has time to go to the gym. She has exercise groups to keep her attractive and slim. On the contrary, married women gain weight because they don't have time to work out. In fact, unhappy married women are observed to gain more weight. A single woman can achieve greater things because she has no responsibility to a family. She has more time to spend in her career. A single woman has less housework to do because she doesn't have to tend to an untidy spouse and children. Furthermore, a single woman can manage her own money. She's not saddled with debts of an irresponsible husband. She's well-rested. She gets more sleep, thus enhancing her cognitive and memory skills. A single woman doesn't have a lot of mental health issues because she only worries about herself. She has time to meet old and new friends. She's not burdened by the demands of marriage and motherhood.

A single woman takes better trips. She can do interesting activities while on vacation. She can also meet more interesting people in the process. She knows herself better. She knows what she wants in life. She doesn't have to explain to anyone why she came home late and who was with her. She has time for herself, her career, and her hobbies. People who are into a relationship have to include that certain person into their daily routine. Thus, they become less focused and less available for activities for self-improvement. A single woman finds her life less stressful. Although relationships bring fulfillment and joy, finding the right man can be difficult. A lot of people who are in relationships find it stressful as they try to keep a balance. They go to therapists to improve the quality of their lives. These people often forget about their dreams and wishes because they focus their energy and efforts in making their partners happy. A single woman doesn't have to deal with such stress. In fact, she can even engage in stress-relieving activities because she has the freedom and time to do so.

This type of woman doesn't have to deal with the constraints placed by her partner or family. She is not bound by the hypocrisy she has to put up with. She doesn't have to spend her day off having lunch or going shopping with her husband's sister or mother when she's rather have time for her girlfriends. She doesn't have to be dragged to the house of her partner's parents for a holiday dinner. She can stay at home with a good book instead of pretending to have a nice meal with people she doesn't like. A single woman's time is hers alone. She doesn't have to fit her schedule with that of her husband or family. She can go shopping or go out to dinner anytime she wants. She can go straight to bed if she wants to. She decides how to spend her money. She doesn't have to prioritize the needs of someone else over her own. She makes financial decisions by herself.

Because she's single, the woman can pursue a career. She can spend long hours to get ahead in her career without feeling guilty that she doesn't have time for her partner or family. She can go on a cruise or a road trip. She can gain a perspective of what she really wants in her life, in her partner, or in her family.

Disadvantages of Being a Single Woman

The feeling of being alone or lonely will usually pop up when the single woman is facing a big problem, going through holidays, or having an illness. If she has no one to celebrate a milestone with or she doesn't have someone to share her secrets, she feels alone. Furthermore, she'll be distressed if she has no dare to dinner parties or a wedding. She also lacks intimacy. As she gets older, she'll find it difficult to find a partner. In addition, a single woman has to do everything on her own. She has to do the household chores, run the errands, and all other things that must be done. Living alone can also be very expensive. If a woman is single, she gets no financial assistance to pay her bills and rent. If she doesn't have budgeting skills, she will experience financial constraints. It is a challenge for her to keep her finances in order. A single woman doesn't get additional benefits in housing, insurance, etc. She even has to pay a higher income tax. In addition, she can't avail of 2-for-1 offers. She has to pay the full price for a cruise or a hotel room. More importantly, she has to take extra precaution. She may be robbed or maimed if she's not careful.

Chapter 2: Saving Tips for a Single Woman

Currently, there are more single women than married ones. There are many single women who earn a lot of money. They now make better financial decisions. However, most of these women still feel inadequate to navigate their financial life successfully. They struggle because they have no formal training in money management. They grow up believing a lot of money myths which caused anxiety, feeling of inadequacy, and confusion. They can't remain in one job for a long time. They usually have careers that didn't offer a lot of earning potential like administrative work and teaching. They have no confidence about the math of money management. They also prefer investing in relationships rather than investing in financial security. Lastly, these single women are often victims of wage and financial discrimination.

It is important for a single woman to take control of her finances because she has to make ends meet. She has no partner to share the expenses with. She has to repay her debts. She has to have insurance and/or savings to continue paying the bills if she becomes disabled, injured, or sick. She is primarily responsible for her retirement savings. Lastly, her future or long term expenses will increase while her earning ability will decrease over time.

Tax Savings for a Single Woman

As a single taxpayer, a woman must plan her actions for the year in order to minimize her taxable income and maximize her tax deductions. She can look for tax savings at her job, her home, her school and other expenses, her family planning, her inheritance, and her retirement savings and investments.

At work, she can work out on her W-4 form if she got a huge tax refund for the year because it means that her employer is deducting a lot of tax from her paycheck regularly. By filing a new form, she can get more money at the time she earns it. It can mean an additional $225 monthly. If the employer offers a flex plan, a single woman must avail of it because she can use a portion of her salary to a medical reimbursement account which can be used to pay medical bills. With this strategy, she can't be charged Social Security and income tax for her account contribution. She saves as much as 35%. She can contribute a maximum of $2,500 to her flex plan.

If the single woman doesn't want to concern herself with higher taxes in the future, she can move her retirement contributions to a Roth 401(k) if it's offered by her employer. The Roth 401(k) doesn't offer a tax break. However, if she withdraws from her Roth 401(k), she doesn't get taxed. If she's unemployed, she can monitor her job-hunting costs so that she can deduct such costs from her taxable income provided that it isn't her first job and that she's seeking a new position in a similar line of work. The cost of overnight accommodation if she has to search outside of her state can be deducted as miscellaneous expenses if the costs don't go beyond 2% of the adjusted gross income.

Moving costs because of a new job can also be deducted from taxable income if the new job is outside the 50-mile radius from her old home. If she uses her own car in moving to her new home, she can subtract 23.5 cents per mile plus tolls and parking. She can also save tax money if she opts to pay tax on the value of her restricted stock as soon as she receives it. A restricted stock can be offered by an employer as a fringe benefit. If she pays immediately instead of waiting for the shares of stock to vest, she can pay a lower tax because the value of the stock may be lower at the time she receives it than at the time the shares are fully vested. The 401(k) loan must be repaid before the single woman resigns from her job. If she doesn't, the loan will be treated as a distribution and will be taxed at the top bracket. She will also pay a 10% penalty if she leaves the job before she turns 55 years old. There are employers who provide educational assistance to their employees at a maximum amount of $5,250 tax-free.

The single woman can buy her first home from her Roth IRA. She won't be penalized or taxed if she withdraws from her account, provided the distribution doesn't exceed $10,000 worth of earnings and the account has been existing for 5 years already. However, the whole Roth IRA contributions can be used as down payment for the house. Educational expenses for training and graduate studies can qualify as Lifetime Learning Credit, which is equivalent to 20% of the expenses or a maximum of $10,000. However, the single woman can't claim the benefit if she earns more than $50,000 a year. Furthermore, she can deduct expenses even if she doesn't itemize them. The standard deduction can be used if it's larger than the total itemized expenses. If her parents didn't claim the interest deductions for her student loan, the single woman can use them even if she doesn't itemize.

If the single woman is a beneficiary of a 401(k) plan, she can roll it over to an IRA account with pay outs stretched over her lifetime. Furthermore, if she has investments, it is best for her to consult the calendar prior to selling her holdings. If she wants to be eligible to a preferential tax rate, she must sell her investments ate least a year after she bought them. Before buying shares of a mutual fund towards the end of the year, she must know when the fund will pay out dividends. If she buys shares before the payout, she'll receive the dividend but she has to pay tax for it, on the other hand, if she waits after the payout, she'll be able to buy shares at a lower price and she won't have to pay any tax. Lastly, the IRA contributions must be made as soon as possible so that she can file tax-deferred returns. If she has a Roth IRA, the returns are tax-exempt.

Chapter 3: Budget Tips for the Single Woman

Creating a Budget

Everyone must know how to budget their money. For a single woman, budgeting becomes a requisite because no one will monitor her finances but herself. As such, it is important to create a budget for a better future.

The first step in creating a budget is to analyze her present financial status. She can do this by checking all her bank accounts as well as all her debts. In assessing his finances, she must include the car loan, student loan, and credit cards. Furthermore, she must know how much she has in retirement accounts, stocks, and other investments. Next, she has to account for her total bills in a month. She can check her bank statement if she doesn't keep her bills. From those bills, she can determine her monthly consumption of utilities and other regular expenditures. Loan amortization is also included in the list. In addition, she must list her monthly expenses on groceries, shopping, entertainment, and other irregular expenses. From the list of regular and irregular expenses, she'll have an idea how much she spends monthly. She can set a limit for these expenses to control her spending.

The third step is to start saving. A savings account is an indispensable way to start budgeting. It should be reserved for emergencies or important and large purchases. According to financial advisors, the savings account must have about 3-6 months' worth of salary. Next, the debts must be paid monthly. The single woman must ensure to make larger payments to her loans and credit cards so that interest payments will be reduced. Finally, she must monitor her bank accounts and adjust her budget if she finds that she's making more withdrawals.

Steps to Create a Budget

It is important for every single woman to determine her monthly expenses. What she can do is list down all her expenses in a month. It is important that she keeps the receipts. She can have the list on a worksheet file or in a notebook. She should categorize her spending into groceries, entertainment, electric bill, gas and transportation, dining out, rent, and utilities. The categories must be listed in a horizontal manner while the amounts must be listed adjacent to the categories. The amounts are then totaled at the end.

After making the column total, it is important to evaluate the expenses. Some categories can be necessary expenses but expenses in non-essential categories must be trimmed down. Each spending category must have a goal so that she can start saving for her emergency fund. At least 10% of her income must be saved for emergencies. After creating the budget, it must be tracked to ensure that she's spending within her budget. There are online applications which can help her track her spending. Lastly, the budget must be re-evaluated if she's not reaching her financial goals.

Budgeting Tools Every Single Woman Can Use

The single woman can still make use of the envelope system. She can use virtual or real envelopes to keep her money for variable expenses like dining out and entertainment. If she has already spent her money in the envelope, she has to wait for the next payday to refill the envelope. There are certain expenses which can use automatic drafts. The 401(k) contributions are automatically deducted by the employer while the IRA contributions can be withdrawn automatically from a checking account. The single woman will only have to make arrangements with her bank about automatic drafts. This method is effective because she won't be tempted to spend the money if it is automatically deducted from her account. Lastly, she can take advantage of money market accounts to park emergency fund. This account has high yield and can be accessed easily in emergencies.

Chapter 4: Retirement Tips for the Single Woman

A single woman needs to make important retirement plans. Because she's single, her financial security during her retirement must be of greater significance. She has to know how to make use of all available resources for this purpose. Not a lot of people plan their retirement. They don't have enough savings to use during their retirement. They don't even maximize their Social Security benefits. In reality, people plan their vacations but not their future.

To save for retirement, a realistic analysis of financial resources must be done so that the single woman can make her most important decisions. She needs to find out ways to cut her expenses in order to save money for her retirement. Some people hire a financial advisor to help them. If she's taking advantage of this service, she has to ensure that she pays the advisor a fixed fee rather than a transaction charge or commission. Furthermore, the advisor must have the necessary credentials to prove his expertise in retirement planning.

Upon her retirement, the single woman will rely mostly on her Social Security benefits. Therefore, it is a must that she maximizes its use. It is important to claim the benefit until she has exhausted all her other sources of retirement income because money from Social Security increases substantially for each year the claim is delayed. The 401(k) and IRA accounts can be used to generate income. A lot of individuals spend their retirement as they please so that the sources of income become depleted even before they die. It is advisable for the single woman to study the different ways to generate retirement income so that she can choose the best alternative for her needs.

Another important tip is for her to ensure that she takes care of her health. Diseases and ailments can be costly and disabling. As such, the single woman must exercise and eat a balanced diet. Although there is no guarantee that she won't get sick during her retirement, she'll recover faster is she's in a better health condition. Lastly, she can surround herself with caring family and friends. She can't be threatened by extreme loneliness if she's in the company of friends and relatives. She can live with friends or relatives to share the costs of living.

Decisions Every Single Woman Must Make

A single woman must make career decisions. Because retirees can have about 30 more years in their lives, a single female must ensure that she still has money to spend for a long retirement period. Therefore, she can plan her career so that she can still continue to work even when she's in her 70s. At her 40s, she can develop the intellectual skills, earning potential, and expertise so that she can still be productive even at an old age. She also has to make investing decisions. If she's putting money in retirement plans, she can decide to put the money in investments to earn more money. When she retires, she needs to replace lost income. She can assess investments based on risk-return trade offs. When she is nearing retirement, she has to make investing decisions. She can't take risk with her investments because she can't afford to lose money.

In addition, the single woman has to decide how she will claim her Social Security benefits. In general, a woman can claim against her husband's Social Security benefits. She can even claim against the Social Security benefits of her ex-husband if they've been married for at least 10 years. More often than not, women are also their husband's beneficiary so they can claim spousal benefits. On the other hand, a single woman doesn't have spousal benefits so the best alternative is to delay claiming her Social Security benefits so that her money can still generate more returns. Lastly, a single woman must decide on long-term care. She must consider being strong and healthy even when she's already retired. She has to take advantage of long-term care insurance so that she can avail of in-home care services later in her life. She can also plan on gathering social resources to keep her company during retirement.

Deciding Where to Retire

Retirement has changed in various ways. Today, couples in their 50s may end up as single individuals upon retirement. Some may be divorced. Others remain unmarried while the rest may have lost their spouse because of unfortunate death. A single woman can choose to retire overseas if she wants to mingle and mix with expats. She can choose a country with interesting people, fun activities, and low cost of living. She must search for places where there are expat communities, events, and activities which help her to stay active. Furthermore, the location must be safe for single women like her. She can start looking for such communities through online forums. She can meet a lot of people online even before she moves or visits the country. She can also search for volunteer groups to help her connect with the expat community and the local people. If she's into hobbies, she can start looking for hobby groups.

A single woman can still date during retirement although she may have a different purpose than a 20-year-old or a 30-year-old woman. She doesn't look for a man whom she can start a family with. She just looks for a man she can have fun with. At retirement age, a lot people already had a lot of experiences with ex-spouses and children. Most of them had failed marriages while others became caregivers of their sick partner. Therefore, most retirees don't want to enter a new relation because they feel they will be obligated again. They experienced physical and emotional losses. Therefore, most of them put up a wall when intimacy is concerned. Successful dating can open up willingness and commitment to move forward even if they feel anxious and vulnerable. A single woman may find it difficult to date during retirement because there are more single women than single men.

In the United States of America, single retirees are often in metro areas of New Orleans and Miami. Most retirees in these locations are single. Divorce rates are also high in the two locations. The metro areas of New York; Memphis, Tennessee; and Jackson, Mississippi also have a large number of single seniors.

In Ogden, Utah, the place had the lowest number of single seniors at 29.3% while metro areas like Boise, Idaho; Lancaster, Pasadena; and Cape Coral, Florida have about 33% of the total retirees' population comprising of single retirees. There are more single women retirees than men because they outlive their husbands. A single woman can move out of her current social network to start the process of meeting new friends. She can go into online dating, attend a new church, or try new hobbies to meet new friends.

Chapter 5: Excellent Finance Tips for Women

Most people live differently now compared to people from past generations. Individuals wait a long time before they marry and start a family. Thus, it is not surprising to find a lot of single women nowadays. Furthermore, because the divorce rate is increasing, a lot of women become single once again. Gender roles can be a factor why there a lot of women who put their needs aside to fulfill the needs of their husbands and their children. As such, they don't consider their own personal finances to secure their retirement.

A single woman must create a budget and try her very best to stick to it. Actually, budgeting applies to everyone. She must assess her monthly expenses without forgetting esthetics, utilities, gas, car amortization, insurance, groceries, utilities, and housing costs. The same must be done with her income. The expenses are then subtracted from her income to know how much is left. The remainder is then divided into her discretionary spending and savings. Payments for debts like student loans and credit card debts must also be included in the list of expenses. Debts must be cleared as soon as possible so that she doesn't have to pay interests on these loans. She has to reduce her expenses in order to have more money to pay her debts.

A lot of women are known to be impulse shoppers. It can be difficult for them not to buy things on impulse but impulse buying must be avoided. Emotional spending must be avoided as well. Unnecessary expenses must be limited in order for a single woman to improve her personal finances. She must make it a point not to use her credit card to buy these non-essentials. As such as possible, she has to stay true to her budget. To do so, she has to wait at least a day to decide whether to buy a non-essential item or not. If she doesn't want to buy it the next day, she made a great effort to stay away from impulse buying.

Unfortunate events can occur in everyone's life. A single woman can't expect her life to be a bed of roses at all times. As such, she has to have money for emergencies. Home or car repairs, or unexpected illness, can be a huge burden. If it's an illness, she may not be able to work for a long time. She need not worry about money if she has saved some for the rainy days. She can start by saving a few bucks a day. Before she knows it, she has accumulated a lot of money already. She can keep her emergency fund in a high-interest savings account. If she has saved for the fund already, her excess money can be used for investing so that she'll earn more money. As a word of caution, the single woman mustn't keep her hopes up. Her expectations must be realistic. The single woman must set a realistic amount for her savings account so that she doesn't sacrifice her other needs.

Every individual wants to own a home. For most people, a home is an investment which can be rewarding in the future. If the single woman is currently renting an apartment, she may think of using the rental money to pay for her own home instead of paying it to her landlord. However, she must first consider if she can afford to buy a house. She also has to think of her own safety. The new home and community must be a safe place for single women like her. She also needs to consider if she'll accept roommates so that they can help pay for the monthly amortization. Next, she has to think what she'll do with the house if she marries and starts a family. To help her decide, she can make a list of what she can afford and what she wants in a house before contacting an agent. She can opt for a town house or a condominium because it is smaller and easy to maintain. Furthermore, it is cheaper than a stand-alone house. She must remember that a condominium or a town house is just a temporary home for her. She can buy a large house as she becomes more financially stable. Furthermore, her needs may change in the future. Thus, she can think of her first home as a way of building equity and establishing herself.

Because everyone eventually grows old, the single woman must think of her retirement even at an early stage. It isn't just short-term goals which define financial security. It is also important to think about long-term goals even if she wants to remain single until she retires. She has to take care of herself. Her budget must allow her to save money for her retirement. Her retirement savings plan can either be paid up using lump sum or monthly contributions.

A single woman mustn't be afraid to invest her money. When she has accumulated cash in her savings account, she can use the extra money to invest in viable investments so that she'll earn more money. She mustn't be scared even if she is not an expert in finance. She has to believe in herself. She can hire the services of a financial advisor or an investment manager to help her with her investing needs. From her initial capital, she can earn more money which she can use to maintain her lifestyle even if she's retired. There are risks but there are also big rewards. She must have the courage to act. She can spend some time researching about investments and pick out investment vehicles according to her risk appetite.

She must not forget to enjoy her life. She's allowed to spoil herself from time to time. She can go on a vacation, spend a day at the spa, or buy something special for herself. These things can be investments on her own happiness and in herself. She needs to reward herself after all her hard work in maintaining balance in her life. Furthermore, she must ensure that such special treats are within her budget. She doesn't have to be deep in debt because of these rewards.

Lastly, if ever the single woman decides to get married in the future, she has to sit down with her partner to talk about money before they take the plunge. They may feel excited about their wedding and forget to agree on essential matters first. The single woman must know how much her future husband earns, his debts, and his future financial plans. By taking the wedding vows, both parties agree to be financial partners. As such, she needs to know if their spending habits and financial habits jibe with each other. She has to ensure that he won't financially drain her and destroy whatever financial success she's enjoying before she gets married.

Conclusion

Thank you again for purchasing this book!

I hope this book was able to help you to become a better person by empowering you to take charge of your financed.

The next step is to try the practical tips listed in this book.

Finally, if you enjoyed this book, please take the time to share your thoughts and post a review on Amazon. We do our best to reach out to readers and provide the best value we can. Your positive review will help us achieve that. It'd be greatly appreciated!

Thank you and good luck!

Check Out My Other Books

Below you'll find some of my other popular books that are popular on Amazon and Kindle as well. Simply click on the links below to check them out. Alternatively, you can visit my author page on Amazon to see other work done by me.

Marketing Money Mastery

http://amzn.to/1hxUaj6

"Debt Free Forever"

http://amzn.to/1qrgldh

Money Management Makeover

http://amzn.to/1hAU8Z7

Single Women and Budgets

http://amzn.to/WPRJ3M

www.ingramcontent.com/pod-product-compliance
Lightning Source LLC
Chambersburg PA
CBHW071826170526
45167CB00003B/1437